Reclaiming Mikvah:
Embracing Jewish Water Ritual

by Bonni Goldberg

Published by Vizye Publications in 2017
First edition; First printing

Design and writing © 2017 Bonni Goldberg

ISBN 978-0-9967524-4-2

Table of Contents

This book is dedicated to Portland, Oregon's Jewish community. Especially M.D. and the incredible women who create and attend Rejewvenation.

Tradition and adaptation are the dual
foundations of Judaism.
Naomi Malka

Chapter 1

Meet Jewish Educator and Author Bonni Goldberg

It wasn't until I moved to Portland, Oregon that I became immersed in Judaism. I'm an accidental Jew, in many ways. I grew up in New York City with two non-religious Jewish parents. I knew I was culturally Jewish, and I had no idea Jews were a minority because they made up the majority of my schoolmates and family friends. I attended a Jewish day camp but only because it was conveniently located. The campers were also very mixed between Jews and non-Jews.

When I went to college, someone suggested I sign up for the kosher dining hall meal plan because the food was better. It was there that I met orthodox Jews for the first time and was exposed to a religious Shabbat and high holidays. I was intrigued by these rituals and traditions that were both so foreign to me and also a part of my heritage. I felt equally a tourist and a native in this community.

I had always lived in communities with large Jewish populations: first, New York and then Baltimore. I arrived in Portland pregnant with our daughter. Shortly after she was born, we moved into a neighborhood that happened to be walking distance from a traditional synagogue. A family with a daughter the same age as mine moved across the street. The mother, Devorah, and I hit it off right away and so did our girls.

The family had just moved from California. As observant Jews, they hosted weekly Shabbat meals at their home and festive meals to celebrate the cycle of Jewish holidays. We were often guests at their table. Another aspect of our relationship developed at their synagogue. Although we weren't members, many Saturday afternoons I would drive over with my toddling daughter, meet the family after services, and join them in the social hall for lunch.

As an older, nervous, first-time mom, I found the synagogue the only place I felt safe letting my daughter wander around with a friend more than three feet away from me. Looking back, it was the equivalent of our indoor play park. My daughter had a little independence from her hovering mom while I enjoyed adult conversation with Devorah and many of the congregants who are now dear friends of mine.

Devorah always used to tell me that I was very unusual in the Jewish world because I came to Judaism without any baggage. It took me a while to understand that she was right. I had no preconceived notions about the beliefs and practices of different denominations. All Jewish practice and belief was fresh and new to me even though I strongly identify culturally as a Jew. Being a Jew with curiosity about all the many ways of expressing that identity has informed my views and teaching as a Jewish educator.

Because of this, I have worked across the spectrum of Jewish practices and denominations. I've taught humanities at a Chabad middle school, run a Jewish Girl Scouts troop and facilitated *Al Galgalim* programs for Hadassah. I was the Director of the Oregon chapter of The Florence Melton School, a renowned international, adult Jewish studies program based at Hebrew University in Jerusalem. I've served on the board of Jewish organizations and written articles and reviews for many Jewish publications. I was also honored to be a recipient of The Song of Miriam Award from Oregon's Jewish Women's Round Table. I'm the author of *Our Family Shabbat Journal*, *My Jewish Holidays Journal*, and *Reclaiming Mikvah: A Guided Journal*, and co-author of the open source curriculum, *Reclaiming Our Jewish Water Ritual: Mikvah*.

Chapter 2

What Reclaiming Mikvah is About

The mikvah is a pool or body of water used in Jewish practice for the purpose of ritual immersion. Mikvah immersion has been a practice since the time when our ancestors worshipped in the Temple. Today, indoor mikvah pools exist in many Jewish communities. To use one, you must schedule an appointment, and there is generally a suggested donation as payment.

It's one thing to decide to reject a tradition or ritual because it doesn't resonate with you or you find it too problematic to adapt it to enrich your spirituality— but it's another matter altogether to lose it by neglect or lack of information. Also, throughout the history of the Jewish people, from antiquity to modern times, our traditions and practices have been outlawed for long periods. Time and time again our people have risked their lives to observe them.

So on one level, taking the time to consider using the mikvah is about honoring those who kept the tradition alive. On another level, it's about trying to understand why it was so important. On yet another level, it's about considering how using the mikvah can support our spiritual life today, to restore this missing piece of our traditions

Chapter 3
Why Embrace This Perspective

There are two main reasons why, as Jews, we should all explore new ways of doing and thinking about our water ritual. First, mikvah is a central practice in Judaism. Jewish law actually requires that a community build a mikvah before a synagogue, a school, or a cemetery. Both a synagogue and a Torah scroll may be sold to raise funds for the building of a mikvah.

Something of such great importance in our tradition that it trumps a Torah scroll should at the very least be considered in a contemporary context. Whatever aspects of Judaism we value most individually, they were passed down to us by the same ancestry that made the mikvah the priority. It deserves examination.

Second, every tradition has its water ritual and the mikvah is ours. In other words, we have a right to claim it and make it relevant to our time and place. It is every Jew's prerogative to choose which traditions resonate. Without investigating our water ritual, how can we evaluate the contemporary value? Why should we potentially miss out on an opportunity for enriching our experience of Jewish rituals? As writer, Amber Keyser says, *As Jews, our task is to wrestle with narrative–to preserve history, to reinterpret the past, and to write new stories that will carry us into the future.*

Chapter 4

My First Mikvah Breakthrough

My first major breakthrough about the Jewish water ritual, mikvah, was profound, and it came by experiencing the ritual itself. I embarked on the mikvah ritual known as the laws of *Niddah* (separation) or *Taharat Hamishpachah* (family purity).

I started out by approaching the mikvah in a somewhat traditional way. As a feminist, I had read some harsh criticisms of the mikvah ritual as it relates to married women, menstruation, and sexual intimacy. I had some vague understanding that the mikvah had to do with immersing oneself in special water. When I was a student in the Melton program, we'd read the Torah and commentary regarding the rules of mikvah use and taken a field trip to tour the Chabad mikvah. I'd also seen the one other mikvah in our community when I accompanied someone who was going as part of the ritual of converting to Judaism.

Despite these exposures, I felt there was something very mysterious about the mikvah. As far as I could tell, it was only being used ritually by married orthodox women, some people who were converting to Judaism, and as a way to make dishes, pots and pans kosher by dipping them in the mikvah water.

Simply put, I wondered why this Jewish water ritual seemed to belong only to the orthodox community. It didn't make sense to me. I needed to understand it better in order to be sure I wasn't missing something important.

For the duration of my menstrual cycle, plus seven days after the last sign of menstrual blood, my husband and I refrained from sexual intimacy. At the end of this period, I went to the mikvah.

In the preparation room, I washed my whole body clean from hair and ears to toenails. Then I wrapped myself in a towel and knocked on the door to the mikvah. The mikvah attendant picked off a couple of stray hairs that were on my shoulders (I always lose some hair when I wash it), walked me over to the mikvah pool, and held my towel so she couldn't see my naked body as I descended the seven steps.

Once in the pool up to my shoulders, I said the prayer printed on a sign above the pool in Hebrew, English, and Hebrew transliteration, dunked my whole body into the water, and came up. Before immersing again, the mikvah attendant said, "kosher," to affirm that the immersion was indeed complete, that my feet weren't touching the bottom of the pool, my legs were apart, and there was space between my toes, arms and fingers so the water was touching every part of my body. After the third immersion, the mikvah attendant held up the towel so that she couldn't see me and I walked back up the stairs and into the towel (I experienced an Ashkenazi version of the ritual. Sephardi customs include reciting the prayer before entering the mikvah and immersing seven times; even among Orthodox Jews there is variety in the ritual).

Afterwards, I went back to the preparation area to get dressed, paid my mikvah donation, and that night my husband and I resumed sexual relations until the beginning of my next period.

From that first experience to each one after it, as I prepared, immersed and dressed afterwards, I was keenly aware of the multitude of women who had been performing this ritual for millennia before me, and the thousands who were participating in it today. It was awe inspiring and transformational.

Perhaps my reaction had to do with my natural affinity with water, or it occurred because the ritual involved my whole body and being, or because I was literally naked and therefore spiritually naked and open as well. It was probably a combination of all those factors and more, but I tapped into this deep and powerful well of feminine energy.

And I loved it. I loved my body, my spirit, my participation in the cycle of women, and my Jewish identity. As I bathed and immersed, I basked in these, the connection to the collective consciousness of women throughout time, and my relationship to that force some name G-d.

I also came to discover that practicing this aspect of mikvah meant that the whole rhythm of my life and my family's would change.

Every vacation, conference, subscription to cultural events, etc. had to be scheduled so that I had access to a mikvah when it was time. I and my family would be arranging our life not around the secular calendar, the school calendar, or any calendar other than the rhythm of my body.

I felt a sense of freedom stepping outside of externally constructed time and into an organic and body-focused experience of marking time. I grappled with my emotions about my body's rhythm as a governing force. This concept permanently shifted my relationship to the societal norms I'd taken for granted as a necessary byproduct of modern life. The natural rhythm of my body was equally important or more so than imposed structures of time.

I was also completely perplexed about how the *Niddah* laws could be interpreted by feminists as a sexist and degrading patriarchal move to further dominate women. It seems the exact opposite to me—a revolutionary Jewish, feminist initiative.

Historically, in a time and place when women were commonly considered the property of men, who could require sex from their wives at will, Jewish men were forbidden that power longer than non-Jews. Well beyond a woman's bleeding days, husbands couldn't even touch their wives. Timing of the monthly hiatus was dictated by the woman's cycle, in effect by the woman herself, not only while she was bleeding, but for a whole seven days afterwards. And only she could signal an end to the separation period, because only she knew how long she bled.

So you have a system where Jewish women control sexual and physical contact with men for a duration of time that the women initiate and terminate, and is punctuated by a private ritual marking their return to the physical, sexual obligations of their (arranged) marriage by immersing in water and prayer.

How can we ignore this as a highly feminist aspect of Jewish society? Would that which some call G-d or a group of male rabbis bent on dominating women through patriarchy impose this: Let's make a rule that Jewish men can't have sex with their wives an additional week every month and let's put the women in charge of when that starts and

9

ends. Doesn't that sound more like a practice devised by women rather than men?

But what about the idea that it is sexist and demeaning that a woman is considered impure, dirty, untouchable during her period? First, much controversy surrounds both the meaning and intention of the Hebrew words used in this context of purity and how they relate to ancient cultural norms: these perspectives are worthy of consideration. But even if you stick with the modern definitions of "impure" as dangerous, unfit or lesser, such were the common beliefs about menstruation among many cultures in the region during ancient times. Even if the only difference between Jewish and non-Jewish practice around women's menstruation was the additional week of separation after bleeding ceased, relative to other cultures of this era, it gave a woman more time and control of her identity outside of the sexual obligation of her marital relationship.

These were the experiences, realizations, and perspectives that came to me from using the mikvah in the context of *Niddah* rituals. They are also the reason I believe that mikvah immersion is a rich and valuable ritual to reclaim in some form by all Jews who practice any Jewish traditions today.

I'm not suggesting that every Jewish woman take on the *Niddah* practice for the rest of her life, but I advocate that every Jewish woman experience some version of it for ninety days: whether single, widowed, in a committed relationship, newly married, or coupled for years, and whether you choose to refrain from all sexual intimacy or specific activities, sexual or otherwise. I do not suggest this because I think or hope anyone will continue the practice, but because I'm convinced that the experience will be meaningful and transformative: participation is the best way to mine the personal meaning in an experience, to find the juice, and to create your own path to honoring what is sacred and powerful in this water ritual for Jewish women. That said, the *Niddah* version of using the mikvah isn't the only way to experience its power.

You don't have to immerse in the mikvah the same way as someone else,or even for the same reasons. In the Torah, there are no references regarding the mikvah about how to prepare, how to immerse, in what kind of water, a specific prayer to say, or that a witness is required. These elements of the immersion ritual were added by the rabbis as Jewish practice was codified to continue without a Temple. But to be meaningful as a ritual, immersion in the mikvah must include elements that make it sacred: to strengthen your connection to the Jewish community as it exists today and as a people in the past, an intention to connect with the force some call G-d, to renew you, to give you strength, and to restore your sense of your innate holiness as an individual.

The only difference between reclaiming our Jewish water ritual and any other Jewish ritual is that most of us lack a context for mikvah. It hasn't been handed down to us from parents or grandparents like many of our other traditions.

Religious uses of mikvah, like other rituals, have waxed and waned over the course of Jewish history. As a result, the regular use of the mikvah fell into disuse outside the Orthodox community, and now generations of Jews know little or nothing about mikvah, much less how it could be relevant or valuable in their own lives.

In many ways, the relationship most of us have to mikvah is as fresh and new as my relationship was to Jewish practices many years ago. You can view this situation as unfortunate, or as an opportunity to approach mikvah with genuine openness to its potential.

Chapter 5

Where These Mikvah Perspectives Come From

After I had my own realizations about the *Niddah* use of the mikvah, I was attending an annual Jewish women's retreat and met the sister-in-law of one of our community members. Naomi Malka is the Mikvah Director at Adas Israel Community Mikvah in Washington, D.C. She introduced me to a growing movement in Judaism to reclaim mikvah as a practice in modern times and for modern reasons. One branch of this movement is referred to as either progressive, open, or community mikvah. The mikvahs of this movement are open to all Jews to use both in traditional ways and to mark important life changes.

I was very excited about this movement. I was looking for a way to contribute to advancing the meaningful use of mikvah immersion in contemporary life. As Naomi and I talked more about our mutual interests, we found that both of us felt it was imperative for all Jews to have access to learning about the possibilities of mikvah immersion in their lives.

The only curriculum for introducing the concept that we knew about cost money—a potential barrier for less formal Jewish groups as well as some formal organizations. We also thought it would be useful to offer a learning opportunity that, while supporting the progressive mikvah movement, wasn't affiliated with it or with any particular movement or denomination. We decided to create an open source curriculum that any group of Jews could access to learn about mikvah and explore its contemporary value.

Our meeting and subsequent discussions coincided with the process of building a new community mikvah in Portland. Support for this effort included numerous stakeholders in the Oregon Jewish community. One organization was the Oregon Board of Rabbis. Rabbi Ariel Stone was the current President, a great supporter of the community mikvah, and a congregational rabbi with a keen mind and commitment to Jewish education. She was also committed to incorporating education about mikvah use in the opening of the new community mikvah.

We were extremely fortunate that she agreed to contribute to the collaborative effort.

It was through the combined lenses of the three of us that the *Reclaiming Our Jewish Water Ritual: Mikvah* curriculum came to be. Our collaboration gave rise to my ideas and perspectives about the mikvah in the time-tested, very Jewish process of study, dialogue, and documentation.

I'm honored and grateful to be part of creating the curriculum, and I hope Jewish groups find it useful. That said, it doesn't focus at all on adapting the *Niddah* version of mikvah immersion into contemporary Jewish life, and that is also an important factor to me.

For this reason, independent of the mikvah curriculum, I've created *Reclaiming Mikvah: A Guided Journal*. It's a more personal and intimate guide for exploring a traditional use of the mikvah by participating in your own version of the *Niddah* process for ninety days. It also includes a section on creating your own mikvah rituals, but that isn't the main focus. Because it is important to me to offer support and guidance for those interested in experimenting with mikvah traditions, I wanted to make the guide to be available to women as part of my contribution to the Jewish community reclaiming mikvah.

Chapter 6

More Perspectives

Traditional understanding of mikvah immersion as the final step of conversion to Judaism bears consideration when exploring modern reasons to use the mikvah. The traditional belief is that the mikvah changes the soul of the convert. As Rabbi Maurice Lamm suggests, it acts as the transition between the convert's old identity and her new one. Without denying or negating the positive aspects of the past, immersion marks the past a "prologue" to one's future life as a Jew.

In the same way, you can enter the mikvah to support a transition that impacts your soul, that marks the end of an older identity and your past as a prologue to your future life as, among other identities, a Jew. These are the times when you leave your old self behind and can't ever return to that former self because something deeply and forever changes you. Such instances will differ for each of us: for example, for some, it's becoming a parent, for others, it's a loss.

In anthropology, liminality (from the Latin word *līmen*, meaning "a threshold") is the state of ambiguity that occurs in the middle stage of rituals, when participants no longer have their pre-ritual status but have not yet transitioned to the new status they will have when the ritual is complete. The liminal state is commonly recognized in most societies, ancient and modern, and it marks a move to a changed status or to a life transition.

In a modern mikvah ritual, immersion is the liminal stage, when you exist at this threshold between your previous way of structuring your identity, time, or community, and the new way, which the ritual establishes.

The mikvah has also been described as symbolic of the womb and immersion as a rebirth. Just as an unborn baby floats in embryonic fluid and doesn't breathe on its own until it leaves the womb to enter the physical world, so, holding your breath, you are immersed in the waters, and emerge new.

If any of these perspectives remind you of the Christian ritual of baptism, keep in mind that mikvah immersion predates baptism and that the early followers of Christianity were Jews.

Chapter 7

Mind and Body: Balanced and Meaningful Jewish Practice

Jewish rituals can be categorized into intellectual and physical practices approached by either mind or body. Most of us are more familiar with intellectual practices such as, reading, studying, interpreting and discussing Torah and Talmud, listening to a talk, speaking prayers, hearing a story, or taking a class.

In Judaism, the mind based practices are balanced by our physically embodied Jewish rituals such as a bris, putting on *t'fillin* and *tallit*, smelling the havdalah spices, drinking wine and eating challah, rocking back and forth during prayers, singing, and lighting candles. One reason for the growing interest in mikvah may result from a feeling of an imbalance between body and mind in Jewish practices.

Naomi Malka explains it best: "Mikvah is the most powerful of the Jewish body rituals because *your body is both the agent and the object of the ritual*. Mikvah is the only Jewish ritual in which your body is both the actor of the ritual and the acted upon. Mikvah immersion is the ultimate reminder that your body is a holy object. The holiness of your body is a central message of mikvah."

Chapter 8

5 Steps To Reclaiming Our Jewish Water Ritual

The question is, Why use a mikvah ritually— for what purpose?
You can find your personal answers by taking the following five steps.

Step 1: Reflect on Water

The first step is to reflect on water itself. In the secular world there is a belief that life came out of water; the presence of water is one of the factors we use to determine if there is potential life on other planets. An adult, female body is approximately 55% water. There is also no new water in the world-- the water in your glass, sink, bath, ocean, the clouds, rivers, snow, the rain, tears, and icebergs has all been part of the never-ending water cycle since the beginning of time.

Moving into the Jewish realm, the word mikvah means a gathering of water. Rain naturally gathered into bodies of water (oceans, lakes, etc.) creates mikvahs. Therefore, at its most fundamental level, a mikvah is a gathering and harvesting of water for a Jewish purpose. In the time and place of our ancient ancestors, water wasn't always so easy to access. Looking to the Torah, at the very beginning, the creation of the world, water preceded creation; it existed even before light.

It's a great deal to ponder: the sum total of the water on our planet has never increased or decreased, all naturally occurring and moving bodies of water made by rain are mikvahs, and in Jewish belief, water existed before the creation of the world.

What does this information suggest to you? Each of us will interpret it differently. It fills me with wonder. It affirms my belief that water is powerful as both a force of nature and as a symbol. It makes me want to learn and explore more.

Step 2: Explore Jewish Relationships to Water

As a second step, consider water in the context of how we interact with natural elements in other Jewish rituals. On the Sabbath, we light fire and rely on the sun and stars to indicate when it begins and ends. During the Sukkot celebration, we live in (or eat our meals in) a hut constructed so that we're vulnerable to all the elements of nature, and every day we shake branches and fruit gathered from the four species of vegetation in the six directions of the physical earth. On T'Bshevat we honor the birthday of the trees.

Fire, earth, sun, stars, and vegetation. Jewish rituals based on natural world phenomena mark cycles and time. They also remind us of the power of, and our dependence on, the elements not only physically but spiritually. Water is one of the primary elements with a significant Jewish purpose among our rituals and cycles.

Many Jews perform *Tashlich* during Rosh Hashanah. *Tashlich* means "casting off" in Hebrew, ritually sending off the sins of the previous year by tossing pieces of bread or stones into a body of flowing water. Just as the water carries away the bits of bread, so too our sins are symbolically carried away. In this way we hope to start the New Year with a clean slate.

Another Jewish water practice is an adaptation created by the Rabbis after the destruction of the Temple: washing hands before a meal that includes bread and saying a specific blessing. In the days of the Temple, the priests had to wash their hands (and feet) before entering the Temple and making sacrifices. The Priests were commanded to use water to mark the difference between spiritual spaces, to transition, and to purify.

Water also appears prominently in several familiar Jewish stories in the Torah including the story of Noah and the story of Exodus (crossing the sea). The first appearance of two of the matriarchs is by a water well. In many Jewish writings, water is a symbol for the Torah.

In Leviticus we're told that entering the mikvah is a ritual practiced before sacrifices made to G-d; before returning to the community after being separated for health conditions; after touching blood or corpses;

seven days after a woman's menstruation ends before a married couple may resume sexual relations; and after spilled semen.

Based on these considerations, how can you make a Jewish purpose for water relevant for yourself today? As with other Jewish rituals, you bring your interpretation to the Jewish water ritual. To do this, ask yourself, which of the attributes of these ways of relating to water resonate most strongly for you: Tashlich (to wash away a past state of being); the Temple Sacrifice (before entering a particular spiritual time); the Matriarchs (to acknowledge being called to a more powerful version of yourself); something else?

For me, there are two: that all water has been part of the never-ending water cycle since the beginning of time including all the tears of sadness, joy and awe ever cried and all the tears of our ancestors and of everyone to be born in the future; and that water preceded the creation of the world. So my interpretation of a Jewish purpose for water is to intentionally enter into the never ending cycle of water to connect with the beginning of time and all of time in a ritual way.

The Jewish purpose of water to which I connect is as a source of renewal. The ritual of immersing in the mikvah is to Jewishly mark the end or beginning of a life phase or situation, to mark and event or a cycle, or to tap into or move into the future with intention, acknowledging holiness, and with respect for the past.

Step 3: Reclaim Our Jewish Water Ritual

If you have a community mikvah in your area, this is an excellent place to start. Call them and let them know you're interested in exploring mikvah use. Resources are also available to assist you with exploring Jewish water ritual that can be found via a Google or Amazon search. Some of the most well known websites are:

⬧ **Jewish Women's Archive's Encyclopedia, under Mikveh**
www.jwa.org/encyclopedia/article/mikveh
offers a lens on the history of mikvah use.

⬧ **Mayyim Hayyim**
www.mayyimhayyim.org
is considered the grandmother of the progressive mikvah movement.

⬧ **Mikvah.org**
www.Mikvah.org - Mivtza Taharas Hamishpacha
is a Chabad site that includes a series of videos presenting an orthodox explanation of the *Niddah* mikvah ritual.

⬧ **The Mikvah Project**
www.mikvahproject.com
is a site that provides a fascinating look into the mikvah experience of many kinds of women.

⬧ **Ritual Well**
http://ritualwell.org/search-results?Q=mikvah
is one of my favorite sites where you can read about mikvah rituals individuals created for themselves, offered to you to use as they are or for inspiration as you create your own.

⬧ *Reclaiming Our Jewish Water Ritual: Mikvah*
www.modernmikvah.wordpress.com
is a free curriculum that explores Jewish relationships with water and introduces the mikvah to groups of Jews unfamiliar with it and Jews who are interested in finding value and resonance with this ancient tradition in today's world. It is structured so that anyone can facilitate it (this is not to deny the value of expertise in Jewish texts,

facilitation, or education) to make the material available so that Jews everywhere, regardless of their resources, access to Jewish educators, or funds for Jewish education, can begin the process of exploring mikvah.

◆ *Reclaiming Mikvah: A Guided Journal* is a personal and intimate guide for exploring a traditional use of the mikvah by participating in your own version of the Niddah process for ninety days. It also includes a section on creating your own mikvah rituals.

Step 4: Overcome Challenges to
Reclaiming Our Jewish Water Ritual

There are two major challenges to exploring mikvah as a personal ritual. One is external and the other is internal. The external challenge is locating a community or progressive mikvah. If you have a local Jewish Federation, they may know. Another way to find out is to ask a non-orthodox rabbi, or other synagogue employee, if there is a mikvah they use for the purpose of conversion or for any other reason.

Here are two lists you can refer to as well, but they aren't necessarily complete or kept current:

◆ **mayyimhayyim.org/resources/community-mikvaot-in-north-america** is a list of North American community mikvahs

◆ **http://mikveh.livejournal.com/2685.html** is a worldwide list of community mikvahs

In places lacking a mikvah open to personal rituals, your search may be more difficult. If there is a natural body of water in your area, you can use it instead of an indoor mikvah.

Remember, you can approach mikvah immersion in the same way you practice other Jewish rituals. If you adhere to a strict form of observance then you may only want to immerse in a kosher mikvah (one that conforms to all the rules of a mikvah as prescribed by Jewish law). If you don't, then even if the only body of water in your area is a man made lake, a pool, or a hot tub you may choose to immerse in it.

The second challenge is feeling intimidated. Some people in your community may actively and vocally disapprove of using mikvah in a progressive manner. You may not feel welcome or sufficiently educated or learned to create your own ritual. You might worry that somehow you would be appropriating a ritual or denigrating it.

You would not be alone in these feelings, but I hope you will challenge them. Transformation, adaptation, and interpretation are at the core of Jewish tradition. In large part, they have contributed to Judaism's lasting power of thousands of years. You deny yourself something precious and powerful when you don't look for personal meaning in this mikvah that our ancestors used and handed down to us, when you don't trust them or yourself to use our beliefs and traditions to make meaning, to better yourself, and to repair the world.

And as a Jew, you have a right to our traditions. You have the right, and some would argue the obligation, to bring meaning and contemporary relevance to our rituals and traditions so that they aren't lost and to help the Jewish people to continue.

If you still have doubts, I encourage you to read some of the mikvah experiences and rituals collected by the Jewish organization Ritual Well (**http://ritualwell.org/search-results?Q=mikvah**); to bring a group of Jews together and go through the *Reclaiming Our Jewish Water Ritual: Mikvah curriculum*; or to take a guided, personal journey with *Reclaiming Mikvah: A Guided Journal*.

If you need support to try the mikvah, reach out to a rabbi, a Jewish group, or a friend. If there is no one in your community you feel comfortable approaching, contact the community mikvah closest to where you live for support. Perhaps you can plan a trip to visit that mikvah and schedule an immersion.

Step 5: Respect Time

Marking time is one reason to use the mikvah. The start of a new career, the end of a marriage, or the completion of chemotherapy are all opportunities to partake in a Jewish ritual affirming transformation, renewal, and moving on from the past.

Time is also easy to let slip by. There may be a transition coming up that you would consider marking with mikvah immersion. But it takes some time to plan and schedule. You may not feel confident that you know enough about it to immerse for your own reasons.

If you let these thoughts take over, you may never find a time you feel is right. A personal immersion experience need not be perfect, either. It only needs to have meaning for you and support your continuing on your path. So, honor time, but don't let it get away from you.

Don't overlook opportunities to reclaim mikvah. Any change or transition, any beginning or end in your life that you need help to embrace, that you want to acknowledge Jewishly—that your soul is calling for a ritual—is an opportunity to consider the mikvah.

Today, Jews have used mikvah immersion before becoming Bar or Bat Mitzvah; in gratitude for an unexpected blessing; to affirm body positivity; for healing; as part of mourning; before a wedding for the bride, groom and their parents; for birthdays; to prepare for conception; before or after giving birth; for in/fertility; weaning; and for milestones such as graduations, moves, retirement, coming out, and important anniversaries. You can immerse to help set your intentions any time throughout the marking of the Jewish year: before Rosh Hashanah, Yom Kippur, Passover, Shabbat, etc.

Chapter 9
A Mikvah Story

Naomi Malka tells a story that moves me each time I hear it. Naomi had just taken over as Director of the mikvah at Adas Israel. She was new both to the responsibility and to her role scheduling immersion appointments. The very first call she took was from a woman who was distraught. "I need to use the mikvah. I just lost my son and my father in the same car accident. I am drowning in grief, and I need a way to wash this off of me."

This woman was coming from such a raw and emotional state. She wasn't concerned with the details of whether she would say a prayer or what it would be. She didn't question her desire to turn to mikvah immersion. She was in acute need and trusted her soul to know what it longed for.

I'm also struck by another aspect of her inner wisdom. Even though Judaism is rich with ritual for mourners, this woman needed something more. Rather than question her need, she reached out for another Jewish ritual. Finally, there is her sense of drowning in something that was overwhelming her and turning to the power of the never-ending cycle of water to wash away this debilitating layer of her grief. I imagine her mourning tears mingling with, and being absorbed by, the water as she immersed her body.

Chapter 10

An Invitation

Now that you've read and considered these ideas and perspectives, it's an opportune time to complete this phase of exploring reclaiming the mikvah with action. I invite you to take these five steps right now:

♦ Think of a transition in your life, either in your recent past or in your future, that you want to acknowledge.

♦ Write down any word(s) that would be meaningful to you to include in the ritual.

♦ Would you want the ritual to be private or would there be participants or witnesses? If so, who would they be? Write this down too.

♦ Is there anything else that comes to mind: music, a special time you'd want to immerse, something you'd want to do right before or after, anything else? Write it down.

♦ Immersion in the mikvah includes going down seven steps to get into the water, completely immersing your whole body in the water, and coming back up the steps plus anything else you want to add. Review what you've written. Visualize what word(s)—spoken or silent—and action would take place at which points. Record this in words, images, etc.

Mazel-tov, you have created your own mikvah ritual. It's up to you whether you choose to use it in our Jewish water ritual as a source of renewal.

Jewish Books and Resources
by Bonni Goldberg, M.A.

For Mikvah
Reclaiming Mikvah: Embracing Jewish Water Ritual

Reclaiming Mikvah: A Guided Journal

*Reclaiming Our Jewish Water Ritual: Mikvah
an open source curriculum
(with Naomi Malka & Rabbi Ariel Stone)*

For Family
Our Family Shabbat Journal

For Children
My Jewish Holidays Journal

Bonni has been an educator across the spectrum of Jewish practices and denominations. She taught humanities at a Chabad middle school, ran a Jewish Girl Scouts troop and facilitated *Al Galgalim* programs for Hadassah. She was the Director of the Oregon chapter of The Florence Melton School, a renowned international, adult Jewish studies program based out of Hebrew University in Jerusalem. Bonni has served on the board of Jewish organizations and written articles and reviews for many Jewish publications. She was a recipient of The Song of Miriam Award from Oregon's Jewish Women's Round Table.